MACBETH

www.**transworld**books.co.uk

The Incomplete Shakespeare

MACBETH

JOHN CRACE annotated by JOHN SUTHERLAND

Doubleday

LONDON · TORONTO · SYDNEY · AUCKLAND · JOHANNESBURG

1   *Although* Macbeth *is the shortest of the 'big four' tragedies, it also has a superabundance of on-stage and behind-stage bodies: spear-carriers in half the scenes, horses (if the company can find a way of getting them on stage) and, at one point, two whole armies and a walking forest. The play is a crowd scene in five acts.*

Macbeth is notoriously the 'unlucky' play – something routinely goes wrong with performances. The superstitious blame the witchery (they don't like being laughed at: do so at your peril). The unsuperstitious blame the fact that there are so many spare bodies hanging around behind the scenes, getting in the way. Too much dramatis personae, you might say.

2   *Why not 'King' Macbeth? No one utters it in the play, either. Why? Think and read on. Shakespeare's theatrical company, by the way, was called 'The King's Men'.*

DRAMATIS PERSONAE[1]

DUNCAN	king of Scotland
MACBETH[2]	king of Scotland
MALCOLM	son of the king of Scotland
BANQUO	father of kings of Scotland
LADY MACBETH	wife to the king of Scotland, co-murderer of the king of Scotland
MACDUFF	king-maker: Scotland and England; killer: king of Scotland
ROSS	secondary king-maker; man of few words
YOUNG SIWARD	killed by king of Scotland
OLD SIWARD	not killed by king of Scotland
THREE WITCHES	much concerned by the kingship of Scotland
THREE APPARITIONS	future kings of Scotland
THREE MURDERERS	killers of the ancestor of future kings of Scotland

LENNOX, MENTEITH   characters with Scottish names in
SEYTON   the service of kings of Scotland

SUNDRIES

DRUNKEN PORTER

SHORT-LIVED YOUNG MACDUFF

USELESS DOCTOR

BLEEDING SERGEANT   (aren't they all?)

3   I.e. Scotland. 'A terrible waste,' said Dr Johnson, looking at
     our northerly neighbour. Why did Shakespeare – who probably
     never went there – go tartan? Perhaps because James I
     of England, formerly James VI of Scotland, had succeeded
     Elizabeth in 1603 – three years previously. Och aye.

4   Did Shakespeare believe in witches? Probably not. Did King
     James believe in witches? Yes. Big time. He was convinced
     they were out to kill him, and wrote a learned study,
     Daemonologie, on the weird sisterhood. He burned as many
     as he could. Do actors believe in witches? They do – so much
     so, they never use the title of 'the Scottish Play'.

5   In no other Shakespeare play is rotten weather so prominent.
     On 20 January 1606, the year Macbeth was first produced,
     Britain suffered its most catastrophic storm to date. The
     Globe's roof, remember, was open to the elements.

6   There are lots of references to 'foul air' in Macbeth. July 1606
     saw the outbreak of a great London plague – everyone who
     could do so scampered out of town and the theatres were
     closed. Jacobeans subscribed to the 'miasmic' theory: that
     bubonic plague was spread by foul air. It was actually spread
     by fleas.

7   Stage performances routinely began at sunny midday. But
     there are references in Macbeth to the sun setting and to
     candles ('Out, out, brief candle,' etc.). Best explanation? The
     play was a rush job for the royal court, upstream at Hampton
     Court, for an indoor, night-time, candlelit performance.
     Makes sense.

ACT 1, SCENE 1

A desolate place[3]

FIRST WITCH[4]
  When shall we three meet again?
  In thunder, lightning, or in rain?[5]

SECOND WITCH ⎯ *key quote*
  Fair is foul, and foul is fair:[6]
  Macbeth shall play truth or dare.

THIRD WITCH
  Do we ever see the sun?[7]
  Or would that be too much like fun?

[handwritten annotation] Summary: the 3 witches are having a 'meeting' - dont know why. - mysterious. - who are they - what are they saying? - why are they there?

8   The bloody sergeant brings with him the dominant 'image cluster' in the play. Blood. Buckets of it in Macbeth. Theatre lore has it that Shakespeare played this part, as he did the Ghost in Hamlet.

9   Historical Fact Alert! History was funny-putty in Shakespeare's hands. In Macbeth he followed Holinshed's Chronicles. Raphael Holinshed was a shameless bender of historical truth. King Duncan was not the old geezer who reminds Lady Macbeth of her father. There was nothing the historical Duncan liked more than swinging his claymore and unseaming some foe like a Stornoway kipper. He reportedly died attacking his cousin Macbeth's castle. Macbeth seized the empty throne and ruled three times as long as Duncan (seventeen years). Far from having his head cut off and stuck on a pike like a toffee apple, he was buried with full royal honours by his grateful people, in Scotland's holiest ground at Iona. Banquo probably never existed. Got it? Now forget it, and enjoy Shakespeare's tragedy (travesty?).

10 In historical fact, they were Danes. Why did Shakespeare change it? King James had a Danish wife.

11 Well noticed, John Crace. Shakespeare more routinely uses rhyming couplets to indicate a character's exit or a scene/act ending. Why? The Globe had no curtains or lights to dim. The clanging rhyme meant 'That's all, folks.'

12 'thane' ('theign') = landholder, in gift of the Scottish king.

13 Duncan may not be as stupid as he seems. You don't want to have blood-thirsty thanes hanging around eyeing your throne. Glamis and Cawdor, as Mapquest will tell you, are 131 miles apart by today's A9 road. Taking care of his estate should keep Macbeth busy.

ACT 1, SCENE 2

King Duncan's camp

DUNCAN

[handwritten: ~ nes littlerly bleeding]

What <u>bloody</u> man is that?[8] He can report
The newest state of war: for I do find
Myself conveniently out harm's way.[9]

BLEEDING SERGEANT

The Norwegians[10] are a fearsome bunch,
But brave Macbeth did have them all for lunch.[11]
His noble sword did smite to lay them waste
And take the treach'rous Thane of Cawdor hostage.[12]

DUNCAN

I never did much like that wretched cur,
Macbeth shall have his title and his land.[13]

[handwritten: Summary :- The King are aware that the situation is serious, they think they may now loose the battle. - But 'brave' 'loyal' Macbeth would save the day... - they won the battle because of Macbeth]

14 *The weird sisters are in the drug and medication business.*

15 *Macbeth and Banquo would have been on horseback – and are so in film versions. The Globe, reportedly, tried occasionally to use horses on stage and, one guesses, confirmed W. C. Fields's iron rule – never act with animals or children. Shakespeare's company used boys for women's parts. Recent 'Queer Theory' has gone to town on the 'sodometries' encouraged by pretty young boys behind the scenes. Judging by the Sonnets, Shakespeare was bisexual.*

16 *'Thee' (or 'Thou') is offensively familiar – particularly to a future king and begetter of kings. Are the witches shaping the future, or merely predicting it? Favourite examination question.*

ACT 1, SCENE 3

A heath

THREE WITCHES
We three sisters do sing and dance
Till we reach a psychotropic trance.[14]

MACBETH
So foul and fair a day I have not seen.

BANQUO
What withered and unholy hags are these
That standeth here?[15]

aimed at the witches

MACBETH
Speak, if you can: what are you?

FIRST WITCH
All hail, Macbeth! Hail to thee, Thane of Glamis![16]

They hail him but he doesn't know them

SECOND WITCH
All hail, Macbeth, hail to thee, Thane of Cawdor!

THIRD WITCH
All hail, Macbeth, thou shalt be king hereafter.

telling future?

The witches are predicting he will be king

17   *The witches can foresee the future. But they are not prophets,*
     oracles or soothsayers (truth-tellers, like he who in Julius
     Caesar warns the big man to 'beware the Ides of March').
     The witches are mischief-makers. Nothing else. Here they are
     creating suspense with their mischief – the 'how's it all going
     to work out' factor. Bear in mind, very few of Shakespeare's
     audience knew the story of an obscure Scottish monarch of
     four centuries ago. The witches' riddles squirm and burrow
     like little worms in the audience's mind until the end, when
     all becomes clear.

18   *'Get' = 'beget'. Odd that we don't use it now, preferring the*
     weak Latinism 'procreate'. There's always a little nervousness
     about Anglo-Saxon words about sex.

19   *Why did Shakespeare not make Banquo a co-conspirator*
     (as Holinshed suggests he was)? Because King James firmly
     believed he was descended from Banquo, via his son Fleance
     (see also note 54). Fetch the whitewash, someone.

20   *They jump through the stage trapdoor on to (one hopes)*
     mattresses.

BANQUO

How com'st
Thou have so many titles for Macbeth
And yet none for me? Speak on, foul visions.

FIRST WITCH

Lesser than Macbeth, and greater.

SECOND WITCH

Not so happy, yet much happier.[17]

THIRD WITCH

Thou shalt get[18] kings, though thou be none.[19]

Witches vanish [20]

BANQUO

It doth seem to me I have received
The shortest straws in these strange prophecies.

MACBETH

I would not lose much sleep if I were you,
For I'm not even Thane of Cawdor yet.

maybe he will be.

Enter Ross

ROSS

Surprise, surprise, O valiant Macbeth
The king hath bestowed on thee an upgrade
And now thou art become a thane twice o'er.

21 *Banquo here plays the part of the so-called 'idiot friend'*
   – always useful in narrative and dramaturgy. Horatio, in
   Hamlet, is another member of the IF club.

22 *Scots and violence go together like haggis and neaps.*
   Holinshed waxes eloquent on the inherent savagery of Celts –
   whether Irish or Scottish. When haggis ran short, they would
   eat each other, says Holinshed.

23 *'Anon' = 'shortly'. Etymology 'at one', or as we say, 'at once'.*
   Note Banquo is already deferential ('my lord') and Macbeth,
   anticipating the sceptre in his hand, lordly ('good friend').

BANQUO

Call me a little simple if you must,
But this seems too much a coincidence.[21]

MACBETH

Two truths are told by supernatural means,
So naturally my thoughts turn to murder.[22]

BANQUO

You seem a bit preoccupied, my lord.

MACBETH

We'll speak anon. Till then enough, good friend.[23]

24 Historically, Macbeth cut Cawdor's head off personally, and sent it to the king. A medieval kind of gift.

25 Duncan's thought for the day. Shakespeare never quite made his mind up as to whether a country would do better with simple honest rulers or with sly 'Macchiavels'. Watch House of Cards (either version) and make your own mind up.

26 The full name was MacBheatha mac Fhionnlaigh. Try packing them in with a play called that.

27 After the real Macbeth is killed, Malcolm will be the first monarch to 'unite' the kingdoms in 1072. Admittedly, William the Conqueror – a hard man to disagree with unless you wanted an arrow in the eyeball – will force him to do it in a conversational exchange which history, sadly, has not recorded.

ACT 1, SCENE 4

Duncan's castle

MALCOLM
> I have report of Cawdor's execution.
> He spoke most well of you and did repent
> When there was still hope of royal pardon.[24]

DUNCAN
> There's no art
> To find the mind's construction in the face:
> He was a gentleman on whom I built
> An absolute trust. Talking of which, here
> Comes Macbeth.[25]

owning up to what he had done

MACBETH
> Thou bestoweth too much honour
> Upon my unworthy name.[26]

DUNCAN
> Think not on't,
> Thou art a decent chap. And Banquo too,
> Though he hath not been given a thaneship
> As reward. Make good speed unto your gaff
> Where our dear eldest Malcolm shall be named
> The Prince of Cumberland, where'er that is.[27]

MACBETH
> Oh bugger it, I had not thought of this,
> Now I shall have to top poor Malcolm too.

28 Lady M's entrance has been withheld for dramatic effect.
    The part would have been performed by the Globe's star boy
    player. She speaks easy, relaxed prose and, where necessary,
    blank verse: poetic iambic pentameter, but unrhymed –
    and where necessary as relaxed as conversational speech.
    Shakespeare inherited this 'mighty line' (along with the
    soliloquy) from Marlowe.

29 A 'monkey's paw trap'. Don't wish for things whose
    consequences you haven't thought through. The spirits duly
    oblige, and neuter Lady Macbeth. What does 'unsex' mean?
    She can't have offspring (heirs and spares). She's later driven
    to madness by blood (e.g. 'who would have thought the
    old man to have had so much blood in him', etc). It evokes
    murder but also menstruation. As Wolf Hall reminds us, a
    queen who can't 'bring forth' heirs is soon separated from
    her head.

30 Recent biographical accounts suggest that things were
    not going well for the Shakespeares in Stratford. Anne (née
    Hathaway) was raising hell about William's carryings-on with
    a local lady called Jane Davenant. He probably got quite a few
    scary killing faces over the breakfast table.

ACT 1, SCENE 5

Macbeth's castle

Enter Lady Macbeth, reading a letter [28]

LADY MACBETH
'You're never going to believe what happened, babe.
I'm just minding my own business killing Norwegians,
when I bump into some old crones who tell me I'm
going to be Thane of Cawdor and King. Stone me if
old Duncy doesn't then make me Cawdor.'
Glamis thou art, and Cawdor, and shalt be
What thou art promised; yet do I fear thou art
Too much of a pussy. Come, you spirits
That tend on mortal thoughts, unsex me here
And fill me from the crown to the toe top-full
Of direst cruelty. [29]
                    Enter Macbeth

MACBETH
Great news, my dearest love.
Duncan comes here tonight.

LADY MACBETH
And when goes hence?

MACBETH
Never, if you have anything to do
With it. You wear your scary killing face. [30]

31 Duncan is undertaking a 'royal progress' – doing the country's
    castles and great estates. Elizabeth I used them to unify the
    realm. Particularly important after a war.

32 Duncan babbles on about ornithology, specifically the 'temple-
    haunting martlet'. Macbeth *is the twitchers' favourite
    Shakespeare play. A country boy, William knew his wildlife and
    there are many references to feathered friends in* Macbeth.

33 And a good guy. A critic once worked out that the ratio of
    good to bad characters in Shakespeare's plays is 60:40. A
    fairly optimistic world-view.

ACT 1, SCENE 6

Outside Macbeth's castle [31]

DUNCAN
This castle hath a pleasant seat; the air
Nimbly and sweetly recommends itself
Unto our gentle senses.
The birds like it, as well. [32]

BANQUO
I do agree,
Then I am dim and unsuspecting, too. [33]

34 *Shakespeare is great on the subjunctive. The point here is that Macbeth is as morally confused as is his grammar. Shall I, shan't I?*

35 *It's a soliloquy. Shakespeare virtually invented the device. Ask yourself the following question: Is he thinking, or talking to himself, or confiding in the audience? Unanswerable.*

36 *The punishment for attempting to kill kings was beyond grisly. Guy Fawkes (remember, remember) had tried to kill James at Parliament, a few months earlier. He was condemned to hanging, drawing and quartering. What (if you can bear to read on) did this mean? His bowels would be extracted and his testicles cut off. He would be half throttled and his innards burned before his eyes. All this in front of a jeering crowd. Resolute to the end, Guy threw himself off the scaffold and broke his neck. We still burn him once a year.*

ACT 1, SCENE 7

Macbeth's castle

MACBETH

If it were done when 'tis done, then 'twere well
It were done quickly.[34]
Duncan is a kind and decent bloke.
Killing him is not nice nor holy
And not at all what he would have wanted.[35]

LADY MACBETH

Have you not topped him yet?

MACBETH

We will proceed no further in this business.
I just can't bring myself to kill the king.[36]

37 *There's a big internal debate in* Macbeth *about what 'manliness' really is: brutal through and through – or 'hard' with a core of tenderness? Bear it in mind.*

38 *One of the great conundrums in* Macbeth. *A bit later on Macduff will say, 'he has no children'. One explanation is that Lady Macbeth is based on a widow called Gruoch ingen Boite, who may have had short-lived children by her first husband. There is, historically, a Macbeth 'stepson' who took over the throne of Scotland when his father died. Niggling.*

LADY MACBETH

    Call yourself a man, you timid thane?[37]
    You are not worthy of my good love
    That floweth over. I have given suck and know
    How tender 'tis to love the babe that milks me:[38]
    I would, while it was smiling in my face,
    Have plucked my nipple from his boneless gums
    And dash'd the brains out, had I so sworn
    As you have done to this.

MACBETH

    Well that explains
    What happened to the child that we must have
    Had and yet can ne'er be mentioned.

39 The term 'weird sisters' is found in Holinshed. The word
    'witch' is mentioned only once in the play. 'Weird' means, in
    Old English, 'fate'.

40 Macbeth is tripping. One of quite a few suggestions in the
    play that he likes his dram (what Scotsman doesn't?). But
    how different would it be if he said, 'Is that a knife?' You
    can use knives for any number of purposes – sharpening
    pencils, for example. Daggers you use for two things only:
    to pick your teeth and kill. Alison de Burgh ('Britain's first
    female theatre-fight director') has given this imaginary
    object some illuminating thought. 'The dagger that hovered
    in front of Macbeth was no slight weapon,' she says. 'It's
    not a battlefield weapon. It's the sort of weapon you carried
    around with you on the streets of Elizabethan England
    and, like a poisoned hat pin in a mystery novel, it's part
    dress accessory, part murder weapon.' No need to ask what
    purpose Macbeth has in mind. One wonders, was Macbeth
    hallucinating a triangulated dagger, designed to be pulled
    out more easily from flesh, or a bladed dagger with sharp
    edges which, when pulled out, would be more difficult and
    messier? The references to plentifully spattered blood, later
    on, suggest the latter. Shakespeare's audience, quite a few
    of whom might have been daggered up (swords could only
    be carried by the privileged) would be more thoughtful than
    we, armed with nothing more dangerous than a rolled-up
    (outrageously expensive) programme.

ACT 2, SCENE 1

Macbeth's castle

BANQUO

I dreamt last night of the three weird sisters:[39]
To you they have show'd some truth.

MACBETH

To be honest, mate,
I have not giv'n the witches a second thought.
But now you mention them, I must concede
You have a point. Yet do not dwell on this.
Wait to see what fate befalls the morrow.

Exit Banquo

Is this a dagger which I see before me,[40]
The handle toward my hand? Come, let me clutch thee.
I have thee not, and yet I see thee still.
My conscience playeth vexing tricks on me.
But not so fast, yon guilt-tripped phantom,
For now I have thee firmly in my grip
I go, and it is done; the bell invites me.
Hear it not, Duncan; for it is a knell
That summons thee to heaven or to hell.
Though most likely, on reflection, heaven.

41 *She's thinking, not talking. The first sign of her eventually fatal mental decline. Macbeth, see-sawingly, gets stronger as Lady M gets weaker.*

42 *Freud – a great admirer of Shakespeare – said he (Shakespeare) had made the great discoveries about the human mind. He (Freud) merely gave them names.*

43 *We still use the term 'lily-livered', although knowledge of human anatomy has made great strides since Shakespeare's day. The Elizabethans believed the human body was kept going by three major organs: the brain, the heart and the liver. It was the liver that took in nutrition and generated blood from it. The 'humorous' (don't ask) quality of that liverish blood created character. A healthy liver would be rich red and its lucky owner 'sanguine' – full of life and zip. A feeble, pale liver would create a feeble person. A 'wimp'.*

ACT 2, SCENE 2

Macbeth's castle, near Duncan's room

LADY MACBETH
    Hark! I laid their daggers ready,
    He could not miss 'em. Had he not resembled
    My father as he slept, I had done't.[41]

Enter Macbeth

My husband?

MACBETH
    Oh what a Freudian slip, 'twixt cup and lip.[42]
    I have done the deed. Didst thou not hear a noise?
    Methought I heard a voice cry, 'Sleep no more!
    Macbeth does murder sleep.'

LADY MACBETH
    Thou hast murdered
    More than sleep, fey and liver-lilied wimp.[43]
    Bless the stars the kill was not enacted
    On the stage where thy vile metrosexual
    Tendencies would be on view to all.
    Give me the daggers and I'll pin the blame
    On Duncan's grooms, who both are also slain.
    A little water clears us of this deed
    Though a large scotch might also do the trick.

44 This scene is a bladder break and some comic relief. The porter is a parody of St Peter at the gates (he rather goes on about that). Odd that the castle has no armed guards. Lady M has probably drugged them. Note that only the upper-class characters can speak blank verse. Characters like the vulgar porter speak prose. Shakespeare is a master of both.

45 The next line, of course, is 'Long live the king.' But who? As Elizabeth (the virgin, childless queen) came to the end of her long reign, Elizabethans debated interminably the 'who's next?' issue. The closest in blood, or the best for the job? Shakespeare was never quite sure. Macbeth doesn't hang about to debate the point.

ACT 2, SCENE 3

The entrance to Macbeth's castle

PORTER

There is a knocking at the door. Knock, knock,
who's there?

MACDUFF

Enough of banter, let me in, old man.

PORTER

Keep your hair on. And your head, the way things are
going round here. Someone's got to have a bit of a
laugh, otherwise we'll all go mad. Anyway, that's your
lot. Back to the action.[44]

Enter Macbeth

MACDUFF

Is the king awake?

MACBETH

In truth, I doubt it.

MACDUFF

I'll go and rouse the royal sleepy-head.
Oh horror, horror, horror,
And yet four times horror. The king is dead.[45]

46 Shakespeare is keen for us to notice what a bloody awful
   actor Macbeth is at this point in his career. This aimless
   platitudinising is doing nothing but raise suspicion among his
   listeners. Lady Macbeth will have to save the day (see note
   48). At this stage – it will be different later on – Macbeth is
   still 'honest', unable to dissimulate. His awful act has not yet
   corrupted him. It will. A query: how different would the play
   be if we actually saw the murder (as in Julius Ceasar)? Did he
   waver before plunging in the dagger?

47 Why – drunk, of course. A Scottish thing, some might think.
   It's not an explanation that would convince any medieval
   Sherlocks. Certainly not the play's 'honest man', Macduff (son
   of Duff, but no duffer). Odd that the Macbeths couldn't come
   up with a better cover story.

48 Does she really faint (the beginning of her descent into
   madness) or is she covering for her hopelessly waffling husband?
   Literary-critical brains have been racked by the question.

MACBETH

My Lord! That is a turn-up for the books.
'Tis well I had prepared these choicest words.
Had I but died an hour before this chance,
I had lived a blessed time; for, from this instant,
There's nothing serious in mortality.[46]

Enter Malcolm

MACDUFF

There is no easy way of saying this;
Your royal dad is murdered.

MALCOLM

O, by whom?

MACDUFF

It seems as if 'twere done by Duncan's staff
Who have not lived the night to tell the tale.[47]

MACBETH

Oh, whoops, I clean forgot to let you know
That I did slay these faithless flunkeys.
Upset was I that they had done for Dunc.

LADY MACBETH

I'm out of here, I feel a little faint.[48]

49 *Union, union, union. Of the two kingdoms, that is. No
    referendum required. Music to the ears of King James and
    his court.*

MALCOLM

   Me too. There's danger in these castle walls.
   I'll bugger off to sunny Engerland.[49]

MACBETH

   'Tis curious that no one wants to stay.
   Some might think Malc had a guilty secret.
   Yet now there is an op'ning for the crown,
   I guess it falls to me. Just fancy that!

ACT 2, SCENE 4

Outside Macbeth's castle

OLD MAN
In all my life I've never seen such things;
Only this morn, a mouse did kill a cat.

ROSS
I did see a foal devour a horse;
Could this be metaphor for something bad?

Enter Macduff

MACDUFF
Now let me fill you in upon such deeds.
Duncan's sons have now fled the bloody scene
And so suspicion falls upon their heads.
Macbeth doth ride to Scone to wear the crown.

50 E.g. see his testicles burned in front of his face.

51 A Scottish thing. Why do they call it 'high tea'? Because it's
    eaten at a table, not in armchairs.

52 John Crace is having a little joke here. Scones are Scottish
    cookies, but the 'Stone of Scone', in Edinburgh Castle, is where
    kings of Scotland are crowned.

53 There are lots of drippy parts in Macbeth. It's one of the
    things which has suggested to critics that Shakespeare wrote
    the play in short order (by royal command, for a July 1606
    visit by the King of Denmark, quite possibly) or that other
    hands than his were involved in its production.

54 Fleance is, historically, the most important character in the
    play. He will escape, marry in Wales and beget the royal
    children who will become James I of England and VI of
    Scotland (James being a commoner name up there). Music
    to the ears of the audience in Hampton Court. Alas, modern
    scholarship argues, very convincingly, that Banquo (and his
    children) never existed. They were fictional inventions given
    currency by Holinshed and Shakespeare. Oh, naughty Will.

ACT 3, SCENE 1

The royal palace at Forres

BANQUO

Thou hast it now: king, Cawdor, Glamis, all,
As the weird women promised, and, I fear,
Thou play'dst most foully for't: yet it was said
That I should have my share, so maybe yet
There's hope Macbeth might meet a grisly death.[50]

Enter Macbeth

MACBETH

How now, my dearest Banquo, don't be late
Back from your ride across the blasted moor.
For Lady M and I wilt make high tea.[51]

BANQUO

Have no fear, I wouldst not let slip thy scones.[52]

MACBETH

Ere you go, may I just check one thing.
Doth drippy Fleance also ride with thee?[53]

BANQUO

Indeed he doth, my son shalt be my sun.[54]
Prithee, why so keen to know?

55 *Macbeth knows them. He has not hired them specifically for this act of murder and child-killing. They are his trusty secret assassins. He killed Duncan himself – but nowadays, well into his reign, he has others to do his dirty work.*

MACBETH

No reason.
I wish your horses sure and fleet of foot.
But if they slip, I will not lose much sleep.

Exit Banquo

'Tis pity I cannot enjoy my luck
And think of creating heirs of mine own.
I dwell upon a future when I'm dead
And Banquo's kids are giv'n all the glory.

Enter two murderers

Ah, there you are, good murderers.[55] You remember
all my instructions? You've got to make sure you don't
just take out Banquo. Weedy Fleance has got to die
too. He may not look much, but he's a nasty piece of
work who is giving me and Lady M nightmares. But
wait until I say so. Understood? We wouldn't want
anyone pinning the deaths back on me, would we?

MURDERER

Your wish is my command, my noble king.

MACBETH

Then go and do your fine and gentle work,
And I shall get my pinny and make tea.

56 It's tempting to speculate that Shakespeare (during the plague-enforced closure of the theatres, 1606–8) was himself having trouble sleeping. Sleep, as he says in Act 2, Scene 2, in one of the loveliest lines of the play, 'knits up the ravell'd sleeve of care' (he's watched Anne mend his jumpers). There may have been a lot of ravelled knitwear in the Stratford household.

57 This is one of the lines in the play that give literary critics orgasmic delight. The 'tender' or bloodshot eye is the red setting sun. 'Seeling' is richly ambiguous. As spelled, it refers to sewing the eyelids of a hawk together to train the bird. Painful. As heard (sealing, ceiling), it suggests sealing a letter with wax (Banquo's fate is sealed) and the roof (or ceiling) of heaven. The Globe had a faux-firmament ceiling over the stage which the actor who played Macbeth, Richard Burbage, may have pointed to.

ACT 3, SCENE 2

Macbeth's palace

LADY MACBETH

    I feel depressed and glum. Nought's had, all's spent,
    Where our desire is got without content.

MACBETH

    I cannot tell a lie, I feel the same.
    The fun has gone out of our deadly game.
    I'm sure that even Duncan might agree
    That he has got the better of the deal.
    For he doth sleep the sleep known to the just
    While we just moan and bicker in the keep.[56]

LADY MACBETH

    Gentle my lord, do try to find some cheer.

MACBETH

    You too, sweet dove, watch out for my next trick.
    Though Dunc is dead, you ain't seen nothing yet.
    Watch Banquo's face at tea. Come, seeling night,
    Scarf up the tender eye of pitiful day.[57]

58 *The on-stage bloodiness shifts the audience's mind from some strange improbabilities in this scene. Would Banquo and Fleance be alone, unguarded (he is a thane, after all) in a lonely place known well enough to Macbeth for him to send his assassins there? Note how in the first half of the play the murders were off stage (Duncan and his grooms, for example); now they are slap in the audience's face. Shakespeare was expert in ramping up the action over the course of the play.*

59 *Shakespeare's stage directions indicate three, not two, murderers on stage. Who is the third? A henchman, or, it's plausibly suggested, Macbeth himself?*

ACT 3, SCENE 3

A lonely place [58]

BANQUO
  What kind of man art thou with such a knife?

MURDERER
  I do what needs be done and that is all.

BANQUO
  Flee, Fleance, flee. Act upon thy name.

Banquo dies, Fleance flees

MURDERER
  One down and one to go. Yet cannot I
  Be arsed to chase. Ride off, boy, and escape. [59]

60 *The large number of castle scenes in* Macbeth *reinforces the theory that the play was written to be first performed in a royal palace, such as Hampton Court.*

61 *The ancestral connection with Banquo is historically murky, but genealogists have reckoned that James I of England was the great-great-great-great-great-great-great-great-great-great-great-great-great-great-grandson of Fleance. Or possibly Malcolm. Holinshed (not a source you would bet the ranch on for reliability) suggests Fleance took off for Wales at this point.*

ACT 3, SCENE 4

The banqueting hall at Forres castle [60]

MACBETH
You are most hearty welcome, lords. Especially you,
Lennox, as I know you are not related to Banquo.

LENNOX
Thank you, my king.

Enter the murderer

MACBETH
Thou couldst have made an effort to clean up,
There's blood across thy face and on thy clothes.

MURDERER
Then 'tis from Banquo's throat. Fleance did flee. [61]

MACBETH
Is there naught thou canst do right, you naughty
Murderer? Read my lips. Did I not say
That both of them must croak? Still, no matter.
Come tomorrow I'll be myself again.

Exit the murderer

LADY MACBETH
Get a grip, thou shaky, shak'n specimen,
We have some guests who give thee funny looks.
Pray, sit down.

62 It's a matter of debate whether Shakespeare believed in ghosts, although he makes fairly regular use of them. What he does seem to have believed in is hallucinations produced by guilty conscience, as here.

63 Eyeglasses (pioneered in Italy) were fairly common in Elizabethan England, and elderly characters doubtless sometimes appeared on stage with them. Twenty years after Macbeth, the Worshipful Company of Spectacle Makers was set up and put the invaluable aids into industrial production.

64 The acid test for whether a ghost is 'real' is if more than one person can see it – as happens in the opening of Hamlet.

Enter Banquo's ghost, which sits in Macbeth's place

MACBETH

But where? I see no room for me.
Banquo is in my banquet seat now sat.
Not that there would be trouble if he were
Because he is not dead. Why should he be?[62]

LENNOX

Methinks thou shouldst have gone to Specsavers
For Banquo is not here, your seat is free.[63]

MACBETH

Thou canst not say I did it; don't eyeball
Me like that, you ghastly spectre. Hold still!
Death is mine; you'll never take me alive.

LADY MACBETH

Do not concern yourselves, my noble lords,
Macbeth doth often have these nasty turns.

Aside to Macbeth

This is the very painting of your fear,
Pull thyself together. You look but on a stool.[64]

MACBETH

You're right, my lady, myself I'm not.
I will try harder not to be so mad.

Exit ghost

65 *Obviously (in Scotland, at least) it's preferable to have a king with a weakness for the bottle than a king who is losing his marbles. Lady Macbeth is certainly in the process of losing hers, but is just capable of keeping the show on the road in this buggered banquet scene. It has put the phrase 'Banquo's seat' (the missing guest) into proverbial usage.*

66 *The central debate in the play: do 'real' men have a conscience, or are they above such petty morality? It's one of the things that make* Macbeth *eternally relevant to the never-ending power game.*

67 *What the witches show him, in their royal genealogical pageant, means that Macbeth will be one of the two most odious child-killers in Shakespeare's plays. The other one? Richard III – like Macbeth, heirless (think Princes in the Tower). Richard actually had a couple of illegitimate children. Macbeth may plausibly have had some as well. But in matters of the crown, bastards are non-existent. It feeds into the creation of the most famous illegitimate son in English Literature, Edmund in* King Lear, *with his great proclamation 'Now God, stand up for bastards!' Whatever the Almighty thought, it took Britain four hundred years to amend the country's cruel bastardy laws.*

Forgive me, lords, I've had a drink or three,[65]
We all have, it's that time of day. Now, where
Is Banquo? We cannot eat without him.

Enter ghost

You're back, you're back, why dost thou reappear?
If scaring be thy aim, thou failest true.
I take thy spectral presence in my stride.

Exit ghost

LENNOX
Macbeth doth not quite seem himself.

LADY MACBETH
Forsooth,
He doth not seem like any man. Pray leave.

Exit Lennox

Don't ever pull a stunt like that again.
If thou cannot man up and be a king
Then all is lost, and you and I with it.[66]

MACBETH
I do apologise, my sweetest queen.
It will hap not again, I promise that.
I take my leave to bother the three witches
And vow to kill whoe'er they should suggest.[67]

68 *Hecate is the Greek goddess of things mysterious. This scene (technically a 'masque') is certainly not by Shakespeare, textual scholarship has decided. (What was it Ben Jonson snottily said? He had little Latin and less Greek.) The candidate for author is fellow dramatist Thomas Middleton, who is sometimes credited with the bulk of the play – less the majestic soliloquies and the Lady Macbeth scenes. The dramatists of this period commonly collaborated with each other – Shakespeare less than most. The fact is, without any surviving manuscript evidence, we'll never be absolutely sure. Best rule: if it feels like Shakespeare, it probably is. And the feel test suggests this scene isn't.*

ACT 3, SCENE 5

A desolate place

Enter three witches, meeting Hecate[68]

THREE WITCHES
How now, we have another witch, why so?

HECATE
Well might you ask, and answer have I none,
Save that this scene was not by Will's hand writ,
Instead was penned by Thomas Middleton.

69 *Lennox, like the two Siwards* et al. *of the original, is one of the wholly thankless parts in this strangely uneven tragedy.*

ACT 3, SCENE 6

The castle of Lennox

LENNOX
I say these lines to make sure you all know
That I too know Macbeth is steeped in hell.[69]

70 *Macbeth* is the shortest – by far – of the four great tragedies.
   And there seems to be a huge time jump here. In this 'Act
   4' (they are not Shakespeare's divisions) *Macbeth* has been
   on the throne a number of years. It has led to the plausible
   speculation that there is a missing fourth act. The plays
   weren't printed (as Folio, then Quarto) until years after
   Shakespeare's death – and then, it is surmised, often from
   impromptu 'prompt copies'.

71 Among their other medicinal services to the community,
   'witches' (i.e. old women who knew about herbs and such)
   were the first port of call for women wanting to procure an
   abortion.

72 *The witches were played for laughs in Shakespeare's day (with
   nursery-rhyme internal rhymes, as here). It was only in the
   nineteenth century that 'special effects' (spine-tinglers) were
   introduced with more sophisticated stage machinery and
   lighting. Nowadays it's the full Stephen King.*

73 *He believes – wrongly, probably – that the sisters can shape
   the future, not merely foretell it. Which, bitch-witches that
   they are, they do with misleading riddles. 'Paltering in a
   double sense' as the play puts it.*

ACT 4, SCENE 1

A desolate place

FIRST WITCH
Into the cauldron goes a frog
And toe-nails of a wretched sprog.[71]

SECOND WITCH
Adder's fork and dragon's tooth,
A passing minstrel on the hoof.

THIRD WITCH
Complete the soup with panda's liver
To summon our desperado hither.

ALL
Double, double toil and trouble,
Fire burn, and cauldron bubble.[72]

Enter Macbeth

MACBETH
Pray, withered hags, look well inside thy brew,
Use thy power, relieve my troubled soul.[73]

ALL
It would have help'd had you not been so rude,
But since you're here, we'll see what we can do.

74 *Riddles again. They help stoke the audience's curiosity – just*
    how is Macbeth going to be got rid of? And what was all
    that mumbo jumbo about walking forests and killers not of
    woman born? He's going to be killed by a branch falling on
    him? Think on, ignorant theatre-goers.

Enter First Apparition

FIRST APPARITION
Macbeth! Macbeth! and thrice Macbeth! Beware
Macduff; he does not trust you well enough.

MACBETH
That thought I'd had already on my own.
Now tell me something that I did not know.

Enter Second Apparition

SECOND APPARITION
Be bold, be proud, be resolute; chill out.
For none of woman born shall harm Macbeth.

MACBETH
This is more like the words I came to hear.
It sounds as if thou hast pronounced 'All Clear'.[74]

Enter Third Apparition

THIRD APPARITION
Macbeth shall never vanquished be until
Great Birnam wood walks to Dunsinane hill.

MACBETH
I like it much, for that will never happen.
Just one thing more; will Banquo's mob be kings?

75 *Why? Macbeth has become very cunning. It would have been easy to have killed Lady Macduff and family secretly. That has become his style. But he wants it to be done with maximum publicity to lure Macduff back in a vindictive rage when, yet again, Macbeth's murderers can do his dirty work for him.*

Enter a show of eight kings

MACBETH

This pleaseth me not. All these damned ghosts
Dead ringers for dead Banquo's ugly mug.

Witches vanish

MACBETH

Saw you the witches?

LENNOX

I cannot say I did.
Came I to say down south Macduff hath fled.

MACBETH

He is a tricky bastard, no mistake.
His wife and babes I might as well now kill.[75]
I'm in too deep to show compassion now.

76 *Complaining wives are an unusually prominent feature in* Macbeth. *See note 30 for the Jane and nagging Anne reference.*

77 *Recall that Lady Macduff, like the actual kids on stage, was played by a boy. Given the unusually high number of women's parts in this play, there must have been a great deal of doubling up behind the scenes.*

78 *Shakespeare's only son died in infancy, by drowning, in 1596. It's suggested that the loss, and the pain it caused, was one of the triggers for his great 'tragic' period.*

ACT 4, SCENE 2

Macduff's castle

LADY MACDUFF
  My husband has run off to save his life
  And leaves us here to take the hit instead.[76]

SON
  Hello, mother.

LADY MACDUFF
  There is no easy way to say this, son,
  But your dad's a traitor.

SON
  Is that all?

LADY MACDUFF
  He might as well be dead.[77]

Enter murderers

SON
  He has killed me.[78]

LADY MACDUFF
  It doesn't sound as if he has quite yet.

MURDERER
  Don't worry, for I won't be long.

79 Union, union, union. Of the kingdoms, that is. Again. The union
    between King and Queen Macbeth is not, alas, going well.

80 Bear in mind that England had just experienced the glorious
    reign of a Virgin Queen, daughter of a king who was anything
    but restrained in his sexual appetite. What rules a monarch
    should obey in this area was a matter of dispute and general
    permissiveness. Which British king had the most illegitimate
    children? It's not certain, but Henry I reputedly had twenty-
    five, Charles II at least fourteen, and William IV ten. Rulers,
    we must accept, live by different rules.

ACT 4, SCENE 3

England, the palace of King Edward[79]

MACDUFF

    I urge thee, sire, to rise against Macbeth,
    Hie thee to Scotland and reclaim the crown.

MALCOLM

    Macbeth seemed honest once, as so do thou.
    How can I tell you will not harmeth me?

MACDUFF

    My lord, I promise thee my word is true.

MALCOLM

    That may be and yet I would remain here
    For Scotland's sake if not for thy entreaties.
    You think Macbeth is bad, but I am worse.
    My lust I can't control and ere the dusk
    I've shagged every woman in my sight.[80]

MACDUFF

    Don't let that stop you. I can live with that.

81 *The 1606 audience would pick up here that Shakespeare is alluding to the sexually voracious and financially greedy Henry VIII. As suggested earlier, have another look at the* Wolf Hall *saga.*

82 *Malcolm has learned one of the prime lessons of successful kingship. Deceit. See his father's remark in Act 1, Scene 4 about not being able to read faces.*

MALCOLM

    Yet there's more, much more, than these
        sweet charming
    Sexual peccadilloes. I am consumed
    With avarice that makes me rob the jewels
    Of every lord and thane throughout the realm.[81]

MACDUFF

    That does not seem too bad. I beg you go.

MALCOLM

    Then know that I am riv'n clean through with sin.
    There is no vice in which I'll not indulge
    My appetites: kids, drugs, drink; think on't.
    If such a one be fit to govern, speak.

MACDUFF

    To govern, no! Nor even fit to live.
    You've gone too far. I will not see you king.

MALCOLM

    My noblest lord, I place my trust in thee,
    For I was just pretending to be bad.[82]
    Yet though you were prepared to overlook
    My heinous sex crimes and my robberies
    I sense thou art at heart a decent man.
    And while you're here, there's one thing you
        should know:
    Your wife and son have met a cruel end.

83 *In the scene in which Lady Macduff and her children are slaughtered, we have a modern (for the seventeenth century) nuclear family. Mum, the kids, dad away at work (saving the world). It's touching. And builds up our terminal loathing for Macbeth.*

MACDUFF

    Why that's too bad, I feel remorse and guilt.
    Maybe I should have brought them here with me.[83]

MALCOLM

    Too late for tears, now God is on our side,
    To Scotland we will go to fight Macbeth.

84 *Compared to the witch-doctoring weird sisters, the doctor is a medical ignoramus. All he can offer is laxatives (rhubarb and senna). Shakespeare did not have a high opinion of the medical profession.*

ACT 5, SCENE 1

A room in Dunsinane castle

DOCTOR
> Lady Macbeth isn't at all well. She's sleepwalking every
> night and her OCD is completely out of control.[84]

Enter Lady Macbeth

LADY MACBETH
> Out, damned spot! Out, I say! One: two:
> The Thane of Fife had a wife. The Thane of Ross
>   was cross.
> What, will these hands ne'er be clean?
> All the perfumes of Arabia will not sweeten this
>   little hand.
> To bed, to bed.

ACT 5, SCENE 2

Scotland. Open country

MENTEITH

The English power is near, led on by Malcolm,
His uncle Siward, and the good Macduff.

LENNOX

Thank you, kind sir, for the aide-memoire
Of all the lords who doth oppose Macbeth.

85 Where have the years gone? See note 70.

ACT 5, SCENE 3

Dunsinane castle

MACBETH
Much time has passed since last I walked these boards,
How much I do not know.[85] I am depressed.
My wife no longer talks, save to herself,
The doc cannot unshrink her troubled mind.
I am alone, abandoned to my fate,
My cause deserted by aught but shadows.
Yet tarry not on such melancholy,
I will be safe, of that I can be sure.
Malcolm did have a mum, I knew her well,
And Birnam wood is going nowhere soon.

86 This is the best explanation apologists for this excessively weak plot element can come up with. It's not entirely plausible unless one factors in that if you intended to lay siege to a castle, you needed very superior numbers. But Macbeth is not fooled. He comes out to fight, rather than sitting the (English) invaders out.

A fellow professor (and eminent theatre reviewer) who kindly looked over this text demurred, in the civil way that professors have (with perhaps a tinge of the venom theatre reviewers keep in their fangs) that – for those of a reflective turn of mind – the ambulant forest was fittingly symbolic: in line with a leitmotif (us professors like a classy word) in the play that nothing is but what is not. The instability of the real world: fair = foul, foul = fair, etc. Irritatingly, I think my critic may have a smart point.

ACT 5, SCENE 4

Near Birnam wood

MALCOLM
Cousins, I hope the day is near at hand
When Scotland will be safe and I be king.
At Birnam wood I have a cunning plan
To cut down boughs, disguise ourselves as trees
And fool Macbeth our numbers are too few.[86]

87 How does she die? It's hinted, a bit later, that she kills herself
    – like Cleopatra, Ophelia and Portia (in Julius Caesar). But
    how exactly did she kill herself? Odd, too, that Macbeth can't
    be bothered to go and look at the body, or, at least, ask some
    pointed questions.

88 Ambiguous. It means both 'too soon' and 'what the hell,
    she would have died later anyway'. This is Macbeth's great,
    soliloquising meditation on the meaninglessness of life. It's
    been an expensive lesson for him to learn.

ACT 5, SCENE 5

Dunsinane castle

MACBETH

    Hang out our banners, I'm ready for the fight,
    Let bloody rivers flow beneath my feet.

SEYTON

    The queen, my lord, is dead.[87]

MACBETH

    She should have died hereafter,
    There would have been a time for such a word.[88]
    Tomorrow, and tomorrow, and the day after that,
    Creeps in this petty pace from day to day
    To the last syllable of recorded time.
    Life's all too futile, meaningless and bleak,
    An existential nightmare for the weak.

Enter a messenger

MESSENGER

I looked toward Birnam and anon methought
The wood began to move.

MACBETH

That's just my luck.
When everything goes wrong, there is still more
That can go wrong. A walking wood is not
What I had planned. Enough of all self-pity,
I could not see the wood for all the trees.

ACT 5, SCENE 6

Outside Dunsinane castle

MALCOLM
  We're near enough: throw off your leafy screens,
  The walking wood has served its cunning plan
  Of messing with the tyrant's troubled mind.

ACT 5, SCENE 7

Near the castle gate

MACBETH
> They have tied me to a stake; I cannot fly,
> But since there is no man not woman-born
> I'll slay the English army one by one.

Enter Young Siward

YOUNG SIWARD
> Stand still, Macbeth, I have thee in my sights.

MACBETH
> I fear thee not, pint-size; prepare to die.

Young Siward is killed

MACDUFF
> My arms are tired from killing nobodies,
> I'll rest my sword until I find Macbeth.

Enter Malcolm and Old Siward

OLD SIWARD
> The castle gates are open, let's go in.

MALCOLM
> That sounds a good idea if we're to win.

89 Ancient Romans, unlike Christians, did not consider suicide
a sin, but a brave act in the face of hopeless defeat. See
Hamlet's wish that the Almighty had not set his canon against
self-slaughter. Shakespeare explores the issue in Julius Caesar.

90 What, the audience will wonder as they file out of the theatre,
does 'untimely ripp'd' actually mean? A Caesarean? Premature
delivery? Was the Macduff foetus removed at the point of
conception and, by the advanced technology of eleventh-
century alchemy, brought to term in a test tube?

ACT 5, SCENE 8

Near the castle gate

MACBETH

    Why should I play the Roman fool and die

    When none of woman born can harm a hair?[89]

Enter Macduff

MACDUFF

    I have not fought with other lesser men

    To keep my sword clean for the greater prize.

MACBETH

    Thou sav'st thy paltry energy in vain

    For thou wert once attached umbilically.

MACDUFF

    That's where you're wrong, thou foul, deluded man,

    From mother's womb was I untimely ripp'd.

MACBETH

    That doesn't frighten me, that is a cheat.

    Caesareans do count. Now let's fight on.[90]

MACDUFF

    The vantage is with me, I think you'll find.

    Thou shouldst have learned to think more laterally.

91 *Just to throw a final spanner in the works, Malcolm didn't inherit. Macbeth's stepson (to whom Lady M probably 'gave suck' – see note 38) did. As mentioned in note 9, Macbeth was buried, his head still attached, in Scotland's sacred earth at Iona. But why ruin a wonderful play?*

Macbeth dies

MALCOLM

    I would the friends we miss were safe arrived.
    Alas, it seems my son has also died.
    Too bad, he'll never get to wear the crown.

MACDUFF

    All hail to me, Macduff deserves a puff,
    For I have killed the tyrant, 'cos I'm tough.

MALCOLM

    Scotland shall be the better now I'm king,[91]
    Its people free of cursed tryranny
    Of this dead butcher and his fiend-like queen.
    Now gather round, thanes, earls, and all my crew,
    I think we've all deserved a drink. Or two.

John Crace is the *Guardian*'s parliamentary sketch writer and author of the 'Digested Read' column, and he writes regularly for *Grazia*. He is the author of *I Never Promised You a Rose Garden: A Short Guide to Modern Politics, the Coalition and the General Election* and also *Baby Alarm: A Neurotic's Guide to Fatherhood*; *Vertigo: One Football Fan's Fear of Success*; *Harry's Games: Inside the Mind of Harry Redknapp*; *Brideshead Abbreviated: The Digested Read of the Twentieth Century* and *The Digested Twenty-first Century*.

John Sutherland is Lord Northcliffe Professor Emeritus of Modern English Literature at University College London and previously taught at the California Institute of Technology. He writes regularly for the *Guardian* and *The Times* and is the author of many books, including *Curiosities of Literature, Henry V, War Criminal?* (with Cedric Watts), biographies of Walter Scott, Stephen Spender and the Victorian elephant Jumbo, and *The Boy Who Loved Books*, a memoir.

TRANSWORLD PUBLISHERS
61–63 Uxbridge Road, London W5 5SA
www.transworldbooks.co.uk

Transworld is part of the Penguin Random House group of companies
whose addresses can be found at global.penguinrandomhouse.com

First published in Great Britain in 2016 by Doubleday
an imprint of Transworld Publishers

A CIP catalogue record for this book
is available from the British Library.

ISBN 9780857524263

Typeset in 11/13pt Berylium by Julia Lloyd Design
Printed and bound by Clays Ltd, Bungay, Suffolk.

Penguin Random House is committed to a sustainable
future for our business, our readers and our planet. This book
is made from Forest Stewardship Council® certified paper.

1 3 5 7 9 10 8 6 4 2